A Picture Book of

DOGS

Written by Joanne Gise
Illustrated by Roseanna Pistolesi

Troll Associates

SAINT BERNARD

Weighing 165-200 pounds and standing over 2 feet tall, the Saint Bernard is a giant compared to the Chihuahua! In fact, the Saint Bernard is the heaviest dog, and one of the tallest, too. But it is very gentle and affectionate.

For many years, Saint Bernards were specially trained to find lost travelers in the Swiss Alps. They led rescuers to the victims. These brave dogs saved many lives.

Metric Equivalents

1 inch	=	2.54 cm
1 foot	=	30.5 cm
1 pound	=	.45 kg
1 mile per hour	=	1.61 kpm

Library of Congress Cataloging-in-Publication Data

Gise, Joanne.
  A picture book of dogs / by Joanne Gise; illustrated by Roseanna Pistolesi.
    p.   cm.
  Summary: Brief text and illustrations introduce twenty dogs including the Saint Bernard, Chihuahua, and Poodle.
  ISBN 0-8167-1902-0 (lib. bdg.)   ISBN 0-8167-1903-9 (pbk.)
  1. Dog breeds—Juvenile literature. 2. Dogs—Juvenile literature.
I. Pistolesi, Roseanna. II. Title.
SF426.5.G58 1990
636.7—dc20   89-39430

Printed in the United States of America.

10   9   8   7   6   5   4   3

CHIHUAHUA

This little dog comes from Mexico. It is the smallest dog. A Chihuahua weighs only about 4 pounds and is about 5 inches tall. That's small enough to fit in a pocket or purse!

BEAGLE

Once used to hunt rabbits, the Beagle *bays*, or howls, when it sees its prey. Its baying may sound sad, but actually the dog is excited. To a Beagle, chasing rabbits is lots of fun!

Beagles make very good watchdogs, and they are friendly and loyal to their owners. Many people enjoy having them as pets.

POODLE

You may think a Poodle looks funny, but its unusual haircut once helped it do an important job. Hunters used Poodles to *retrieve*, or fetch, birds from the water. The thick fur on its legs was shaved off to help the dog swim faster, but the fur on its chest and head was left to keep the Poodle warm in the chilly water.

Poodles come in 3 sizes. Standard Poodles are the biggest, over 15 inches tall. Miniature Poodles are between 10-15 inches tall. The smallest Poodle, called a Toy Poodle, is under 10 inches tall. Poodles are thought to be the smartest of all dogs.

BASENJI

Did you know there is a kind of dog that cannot bark? The Basenji (buh-SEN-gee) can't! Instead it makes a whining noise that sounds a bit like a yodel. The Basenji is also the only dog that washes itself like a cat.

This dog originally came from Africa about 5000 years ago. Because the Basenji can run very fast, it was used in Africa to hunt antelope. Now it makes a good pet for people who want a *very* quiet dog.

GERMAN SHEPHERD

The German Shepherd is very smart and easy to train. It is a very loyal pet and friend. But for many people, this dog is more than just a pet. It has been used as a guard dog, a guide for the blind, a helper to the police, and much more. One of the most popular breeds of dog, the German Shepherd was originally bred to herd sheep and cattle in its native Germany. Now it helps people in many other ways.

DALMATIAN

The Dalmatian is the fireman's mascot. Back in the days when fire trucks were pulled by horses, Dalmatians would run between the wheels to keep the horses company. Often they would run ahead to clear the streets so the truck could get through quickly.

The black and brown spots that make a Dalmatian so easy to recognize don't show up until the puppies are about a month old. They are pure white when they are born.

PEKINGESE

Long ago, only the royal family of China could own Pekingese. If one was stolen, the thief could be put to death. These dogs even had their own servants to care for them! Because it is a small dog—it only weighs 6-10 pounds— women used to carry Pekingese in their sleeves to keep their hands warm!

Pekingese lived in China for hundreds of years, but no one outside of that country ever saw one. Then, in 1860, a British soldier brought several of them to England. It soon became one of the most popular dogs in the world.

The Pekingese is very brave. Even though it is not a big dog, it will attack anything that it thinks will hurt its owner.

DACHSHUND

The legs of this little dog seem to be much too short for its body. Sometimes it is called ''the frankfurter dog''! Because of its shape, it was once used to dig badgers out from their underground tunnels. ''Dachshund'' is German for ''badger dog.''

COLLIE

The Collie's long, thick coat is very beautiful, but it is very helpful, too. For hundreds of years, the Collie has been used to guard and herd sheep. Its thick fur helps keep it warm and dry in any kind of weather.

LABRADOR RETRIEVER and GOLDEN RETRIEVER

Both of these dogs are used by hunters to retrieve birds from the water. Their thick, water-resistant coats keep them warm and dry when they swim—something they love to do.

The Labrador originally came from Canada. The Golden Retriever came from Scotland. Both dogs are friendly, very smart, and easy to train. For these reasons, they are often used as guide dogs for the blind.

SIBERIAN HUSKY

In the cold Arctic, people once depended on dogs for transportation. Teams of dogs pulled sleds that carried people and supplies from place to place. The Siberian Husky was one of the best dogs for this job. Standing almost 2 feet tall, the Husky is very strong and quick.

This dog's special coat also helped it live and work in the Arctic's chilly climate. Its thick coat is actually 2 coats. The outer coat is smooth and helps the dog stay dry. The inner coat is soft and warm to keep out the freezing air.

Huskies were also used in their native Siberia to herd animals. Nowadays they make good pets for families all over the world.

COCKER SPANIEL

The Cocker Spaniel belongs to a group of dogs called *sporting dogs.* It got its name because it was once used to hunt birds called *woodcocks.* It is the smallest of the sporting dogs. Today, it is no longer used for hunting. But its small size and beautiful, feathery coat make the Cocker Spaniel a very popular house pet.

SMOOTH FOX TERRIER

Fox hunting was a very popular sport in England in the mid-1800s. The Fox Terrier was bred especially for this sport. With its good eyesight and sense of smell and its ability to run fast, this dog was very good at chasing foxes. It is called "smooth" because it has a smooth, short-haired coat.

The Fox Terrier has a lot of energy and loves to play. It is a fun and loving pet.

ENGLISH SETTER
and POINTER

These two dogs are a big help to hunters. Their excellent sense of smell helps them find animals or birds hiding in the bushes. When they smell their prey, these dogs stand very still and *point* toward the animal by looking in that direction. Sometimes they lift one front paw, too. This shows the hunter where the prey is hiding. "Pointing" gave the Pointer its name.

The English Setter has a long, silky coat. Long hair, called *feathers,* covers its legs and tail. The Pointer has a short-haired coat.

MALTESE

This little dog's pure white coat is so long it sometimes trails along on the ground. This breed is often called "the world's first lap dog." It is over 2000 years old! Ladies in ancient Greece and Rome were so fond of these dogs, they treated them like babies. Now this is one of the most gentle dogs—but it likes to be spoiled!

CAIRN TERRIER

This lively little dog got its name because it used to dig under *cairns*, or piles of stones, to catch rats and other animals. It comes from the Highlands of Scotland. A loving and friendly pet, it is also a good watchdog, in spite of its small size.

GREYHOUND

Most dogs hunt by using their noses to smell their prey. But the Greyhound runs so quickly it can keep its prey in sight. It is the fastest dog. A Greyhound can run as fast as 40 miles an hour! Some people even go to Greyhound races and watch these slim, smooth-coated dogs chase a mechanical rabbit down a track.

Along with being the fastest dog, the Greyhound is also one of the oldest. Drawings of this dog have been found in the ruins of ancient Egypt.